Discard

# Nothing But the Truth

ALLISON TRUE

authorHOUSE®

*AuthorHouse*™
*1663 Liberty Drive*
*Bloomington, IN 47403*
*www.authorhouse.com*
*Phone: 1-800-839-8640*

*Published by AuthorHouse    01/09/2015*

*ISBN: 978-1-4969-3905-0 (sc)*
*ISBN: 978-1-4969-3906-7 (e)*

# CONTENTS

Preface ............................................................................... ix

Chapter 1    The Setting ........................................................ 1

Chapter 2    The Facility before I Arrived ............................. 7

Chapter 3    My Hire and Directives ..................................... 11

Chapter 4    Therapy Cuts ..................................................... 17

Chapter 5    Mabel and Her Termination ............................ 27

Chapter 6    Mabel's Revenge ............................................... 37

Chapter 7    A Community of Enablers ................................ 41

Chapter 8    A Special Board Meeting Regarding a Complaint .......... 47

Chapter 9    Skip Walton's Recall ........................................ 55

Chapter 10   Chief of Police Jed Poorman ........................... 59

Chapter 11   My Lawsuit ....................................................... 65

Chapter 12   Staff Sabotage ................................................. 69

Chapter 13   Board Meeting with Mob ................................ 73

Chapter 14   My Last Day and Termination ......................... 77

Chapter 15   What I Had Discovered .................................... 81

Chapter 16   Now as I Look Back .......................................... 85

Conclusion .......................................................................... 89

# NOTHING BUT THE TRUTH

Living in this town is like living in the Twilight Zone. The people walk around dressed in the garb of the time. They smile and greet you and help you gather what you might have dropped.

# PREFACE

Anyone could write a story such as this since we have all been unjustly treated once. So in writing this, I am hoping to be a voice for those who have such stories and help them—and their stories—feel better.

I grew up on a farm in northern Minnesota. My father, Adam Douglas, cultivated sugar beets and small grains on his farm. By the time I was ten, I worked as hard and as long as the hired men on the farm. Working side by side with and for my father, I was the recipient of all kinds of sage advice. Whenever a glitch or difficulty arose—and that was just about every day—my father was quick to remind me that everyone has problems, some of them huge.

"Olivia," he would say, "it's how you react to and problem-solve that will define you as a person."

My career path took me through many venues. I started out as a social worker. During that time, I went back to college to pursue a teaching degree. After teaching for a couple of years, I entered the health-care industry as a human resources manager. After two years, I obtained my nursing home administrator's license and became the boss.

Sometimes being the boss requires making tough decisions. During my tenure as a nursing home administrator, I encountered an employee who had been guilty of a number of policy violations for nearly twenty years. She falsified overtime reports to the facility. During tax season work hours, she ran a tax-preparing business from her office in the facility. Most of her clients were employees there, and they all stayed on the clock.

There were many such things. The worst was that during her necessary overtime, she would move around the building and spread rumors and lies about people she wanted to ruin. There was always someone. It was *bad* to cross her.

She was quite invested in convincing staff and family members that she was really the chief authority of the building. She wanted people to believe she was endowed with the authority to run the facility. Many times after she left I found in her papers bills where she had gushingly added a note asking a folksy question about a child who made the honor roll or scored a winning touchdown. She would inquire about a sick family member or offer super sweet sympathies if there had been a death. She was using her position and opportunities to correspond on behalf of the facility to build a fan base. The positive feedback they would offer was feeding into her narcissism.

Her name is Mabel Bitters. Upon her termination, she vowed to get even with me. She simply, in her mind, couldn't be wrong. She believed she was the one who had been wronged. There were reports I got from the community that she would sit in bars and brag that she would triumph in the end.

There are other themes to the story. It begins with Mabel's extraordinary ability to hold a grudge against someone whom she believes to have harmed her in some way.

Mabel is very skilled at identifying people who would believe everything she tells them. The nastier the gossip she fed them, the better and the more they liked it.

A key component of her gossip strategy was to write personal letters to the community. In these letters, she tattled on the people she wanted to hurt. She had credibility and no one really understood how she had won it.

Rumors around town reported that she had withdrawn her twenty-year state pension to spend on legal pursuit of revenge on me.

Gossip had fueled the scandal and the downfall of a former administrator and director of nursing and, now, of course, me. These people had been gossips all their lives. It was not difficult for her to spread enough dirt about people that was eagerly received. No one's reputation was safe. And they were persistent. This tactic had worked before to destroy others. Even people who were skeptical or dismissive at first were eventually worn down. This letter writing/gossip strategy had worked successfully on a former administrator and Director of Nursing.

They spent lots of time together; sometimes behind closed doors in the administrator's office. Both of them were making it easy for people to wonder what was going on. Mabel's office was next to the administrator. Mabel started the rumor that they were having an affair. Skip, the chairman of the board, told me that she wrote board members about the affair.

The rumor campaign went on for nine months.

The administrator had a 17 year tenure. He was well liked by the Board Skip told me. The staff liked him because he never enforced policies or disciplined anyone enabling bad behavior for years. His timidity gave rise, I and others believe, to Ruff Riders, a group of employee bullies, and chronic poor attendance by others. This is a huge expense for the facility because replacing the absent employee usually at the cost of overtime. The Ruff Riders drove out many new employees. Recruiting, hiring and training of new staff is very costly.

Eventually, they were fired and walked out of the building. Both people have found jobs elsewhere and they are both still married to their spouses.

*Never put off writing until you are better at it.*

—Gary Henderson

# CHAPTER 1

## THE SETTING

Tucked in southeastern Minnesota is a small town named Red Bud. It is primarily a rural community with the values of hard work, hard play, and relationships that have been solid since kindergarten.

It is a lovely area. The colors of southeastern Minnesota are spectacular.

In the spring, everything is green, and flowers are everywhere. It is a rainbow of color. The smell of cut alfalfa pervades the air.

In the summer, everything is still green. The flower display continues, and you can smell wonderful things everywhere. Because it is a hilly, roly-poly terrain the panoramic vistas are captivating. One never gets used to them or takes them for granted.

In the fall, the leaves change color and only enhance the views of the valleys and vistas.

In the winter, all is blanketed in white contrasting with patches of black dirt which the snow doesn't cover. On sunny days, and there are many, it looks like diamonds glistening against the snow. The trees are frosted with snow, and one alone is a work of art.

The culture of Red Bud revolved around recreation. They played golf or camped. The county had a trail designed to accommodate four-wheeled vehicles in regular weather and snowmobiles in the winter. In the summer, there were also stock-car races. All summer long, there were sporting events for students of all ages. Often, they lasted all weekend. This all perpetuated the bringing of people together in groups—groups that were acceptable and groups that were not.

Each holiday or notable day, there was a parade. They all contained the same exhibits, such as old farm implements and every fire truck in the county. There also was a group known as "the anarchists." They rode motorcycles and generally attracted a lot of attention. They funded many civic activities and helped lots of philanthropic efforts. A gathering of them all was Red Bud's own Duck Dynasty. The weekends were so scheduled with fun activities that everyone was busy. Thus, for many, there was little or no time for worship or church.

Behind this veil of sweet Midwestern values and culture was a community that eats its young and destroys one another when they want to. The disguise is well maintained.

But none of this is like living there among them idyllic as it may sound.

Now, sometimes someone who grew up in this town and moved away but comes back to retire or care for a relative can slip right back in as if he had never left. Even though that person had moved away, he is still considered an "innie."

I, on the other hand, was an "outie." No matter what I did, it would be scrutinized, criticized, written about in the paper, discussed at church suppers, fodder for the courthouse employees, and reasons for people with nothing to do but to write nasty letters to county board members, important local officials, and state survey officials.

People who had lived in Red Bud their entire lives were criticized and often the target of gossip. But they were always forgiven when the drama passed.

For example, the local judge murdered an attorney who was going to run against him in the next election. He crept into the legal office and murdered the attorney there. However, it was the partner of the intended target. The wrong man was killed. The family was not censured in every way. I spent a long time interviewing the detective who investigated the crime. It was the wife who called the police when her husband returned.

The murder was covered well in the papers and a made for TV movie.

When I arrived at the facility the judge's wife was the story lady for the facility. She came in weekly to read a chapter of a book to the residents.

*This town has a different way of handling things.*
                        —Norman Bates on *The Bates Motel*

# CHAPTER 2

## THE FACILITY BEFORE I ARRIVED

The county in which I lived owned a nursing home named Peaceful Acres, which was losing $75,000 a month, or about a half million dollars a year. The discussion was, prior to my arrival, to sell the building or pass a voter referendum to continue to subsidize the home at a half a million dollars a year for three years.

If the facility were to be purchased, there were two major concerns. The first concern was that the building was constructed in the 1960s and any new owner would need to spend thousands to bring it up to code. The current building was three levels tall. In a fire or weather emergency, it would be a huge concern to keep residents safe or even evacuate them. The building was also extremely energy-inefficient. Things in general were poorly maintained because there were no funds available for normal, routine upkeep. Only emergencies were addressed.

While this is typical of many businesses, it is a very poor business practice. Ideally, there should be a preventative maintenance program in place that includes regularly scheduled maintenance and monitoring for replacement when repair costs reach a certain established benchmark.

The facility had none of these in place, and I did what I could to establish an infrastructure list and anticipate replacement of equipment based on age and repair costs.

The other concern was that a potential buyer would take the bed license and use it to add on to an existing property or build somewhere else in a less remote region. New nursing home beds are not being given out in Minnesota or many other states. The government realizes nursing home care is expensive. This was the case in the government-owned home, Peaceful Acres, since the union wages and the Medicare and Medicaid reimbursement available didn't cover the benefits that the union wages demanded.

If the buyer bought the beds (called a Certificate of Need), this would mean loss of employment for many people who have few skills to get hired elsewhere. And the residents would be placed in another facility in a neighboring community, causing travel hardships for elderly spouses and friends when visiting.

Fortunately for Peaceful Acres, the referendum passed in 2009. All this did was to give the facility a short reprieve. Peaceful Acres now had three years to get its financial house in order as the referendum was set to expire in October, 2012.

*Just go out there and do what you have to do.*

—Martina Navratilova

# CHAPTER 3

## My Hire and Directives

Thus, when I was hired, the first directive I was given was to determine and correct the causes of the financial problems. I was asked during the interview process how long it would take for me to analyze the financial issues. My response was, "Not long; a review of a few months of profit and loss statements and a study of operations would do the trick." As it turned out, it took fewer than two weeks. My review led me to conclude that all departments were overstaffed. No department heads even knew their budget and therefore kept no spend-down sheets or financial records. Long-term department heads commented that they had never been given a budget to follow. So naturally, they just spent.

Also, there were long-time practices that had caused financial burden on the facility. For example it did the laundry for the jail and a local dentist. It cooked all the meals for the jail at a ridiculous charge. While the meals cost over $8.50 to make, the jail was only charged $7.50. To make matters worse, the facility had to pay overtime wages for employees to deliver these meals on the weekends. The largest financial burden on the facility, however, was due to the fact that about half of the staff at Peaceful Acres had twenty-plus years' seniority and made half again their hourly wage in benefits. Additionally, the facility did all the meals-on-wheels cooking for the state nutrition program site meals and the local day care! While some of these agencies received government funding to offset their costs, in the end, they kept all of the funds for themselves. The facility billed strictly by the meal, which did not cover its costs. The mere suggestion that this was unfair to the facility was not received very well, to say the least.

The other directive I was given was to enforce the disciplinary policies. There was a group known around the area as the "Ruff Riders." They had worked there for thirty years and were quite simply bullies with no respect for authority who used sneaky tactics to get their way. They did not do their evil in public where they could get in trouble. They worked behind-the-scenes and filled family members with misinformation. Had they been caught, they would not have been stopped. There had been a series of weak administrators who turned a blind eye to infractions of the rules. It was just easier. Members of the Ruff Riders were well connected in town. For example, one of them was married to one of the sheriff's deputies in town. He was married to Eunice Robinson who was a leader in the Ruff Riders. Another was married to a member of the county board.

Members of the Ruff Riders acted much like home invaders. They could circle you and say mean things, punch you, or torment in any number of ways. Gossip was a favorite tool. Bullying was standard practice. One nurse aid was targeted by the bullies. Finally she was so nervous she said to me that she did not want to come to work, or maybe quit. I spoke with her doctor and suggested she give the nurse aid a leave of absence. This would give her a rest and time to decide if she wanted to continue her employment. The doctor agreed with me and she did return after the leave comforted that I had her best interests at heart.

The sheriff was John Wright, and he covered for Robinson the chief deputy over the years. I was told that Robinson took his family to St. Paul in a squad car, and when he got reported for it, Wright said he had given him permission to do so. It's like the whole town was afraid of the Robinsons. They had bullied people for decades. Those who protested were harassed by law enforcement. One of the nurse aides remarked that she had been followed home by a squad car at night.

Whenever any discipline was attempted against any of the Ruff Riders, they would deny any culpability. The burden of proof then fell on the supervisor. The supervisors were afraid of them too and did nothing.

The administrator before me once tried to discipline Eunice Robinson. Eunice went to the union to grieve it, and when the administrator and staff were supposed to meet with Eunice to discuss her grievance, she brought in her husband and two adult sons and together they tried to get her to drop it. When she didn't, her tires were slashed and sugar was put in her gas tank. Even when her tires were slashed a second time, she never reported it to the authorities. All that muscle was meant to intimidate.

One day, Deputy Robinson came to see me. He wanted to file a complaint about one of Eunice's victims harassing her. He wanted me to know that if I didn't do something about it, he would file a complaint against me for not doing anything and allowing a hostile work environment. His wife and her cohorts created a hostile work environment every day. New employees were driven out. Good employees were harassed.

Prior to that conversation with Deputy Robinson, I had asked my Human Resources Manager, Candy Sheaves, to sit in and take notes. Fact was, I was afraid to be alone with him. After Candy left, he threatened me with a harassment lawsuit, since he had reported that his wife was being bullied. I told him if anything happened to my car or me, I was going straight to the state police and the attorney general.

After that, I called the chairman of the county board, and he said he would call Robinson and tell him he better not hurt me or my car, which I appreciated. His name was Skip Walton, and he knew Eunice was the leader of the Ruff Riders, as some people called them. Skip later told me that he had had two vehicles destroyed with sugar in the gas tank. He had installed locks on the all of the rest of his gas tanks.

*The past cannot be cured.*

—Queen Elizabeth I

# CHAPTER 4

## THERAPY CUTS

Financially, the first thing I realized was that the facility needed more revenue. While there are a variety of ways for a nursing home to increase its revenue, my thirteen years of experience as an administrator had taught me that the most significant increases, as well as the most immediate, would come through the therapy department.

The way the nursing home business works is real revenue is generated by skilled therapies. The Medicare rules are very specific and are driven by minutes of therapy delivered and supported by the patient-making progress. Each patient assessment generates a RUG score (Resource Utilization Group), and each score is connected to a reimbursement rate. So one wants as high of a score as possible. Each score required a certain amount of therapy minutes.

For over twenty years, the hospital therapists had provided the therapy to the nursing home. While they charged by the hour, they included in their hours the time they went on break and to the bathroom. This is not how Medicare works, and they had no knowledge of the system. The reimbursement is determined by minutes of therapy delivered.

For all practical purposes, the hospital therapists drove the facility's census. They decided when people got discharged having reached their therapy goals. In long-term care, this is supposed to be an interdisciplinary decision based on the level of function and when care-plan goals have been met. In my experience, no one was discharged without the administrator's say-so. That came after asking many clinical questions to decide what was in the best interest of the resident. Generally, the administrator decides who gets admitted and discharged. Medicare meetings are held to discuss clinical issues.

The hospital therapists also refused to work with any resident who was demented or made slow or sporadic progress. They had no understanding of how the elderly heal, and they wouldn't be told.

I quickly realized that it was imperative to switch therapy companies. There were many companies out there who specialized in nursing homes. They understood the reimbursement system, and if it took coming in on the weekend to get the minutes, they would need to make the RUG score. In fact, reimbursement is based on assessment, and the assessment drove how many minutes of therapy will be reimbursed.

This was not going to be easy. This was going to be a major war. First, the therapists had worked there for over twenty years. The hospital was a shrine in the community. The doctors did not want anyone in the local health-care circle criticized. Everything was fine the way it was.

To try to get the ball rolling on this potential increase in revenue for the facility, I met with the therapy director, Debbie Montgomery, from the hospital. I had outlined with her the typical expectations of a nursing home administrator. From the course of the conversation, it became apparent that she didn't think she worked for me. She thought I worked for her! Productivity reports are standard throughout businesses of all kinds.

She said, "Oh, we don't do those."

I commented that changes in the reimbursement process meant therapists would have to come in on weekends to capture the required minutes.

She replied, "Oh, we won't be doing that."

This was not an optional response. In order to get revenue, it had to be done.

Following that sad and unproductive meeting, Debbie sent me a bill for $60.00! I had never paid for a consultation with a therapy director in my professional career. The therapists are usually glad to get the business. However, their revenue did not come from Medicare. It came from the nursing home. So revenue we could have been garnering from Medicare for the last twenty years was forever gone. That's millions of dollars over twenty years. These therapists treated the residents for a few days and sent them home. Elderly people recovered like a roller coaster. These therapists expected people to recover in a straight line.

And it wasn't just the revenue. The residents paid into Medicare all of their lives, and they were now sick and in need of their benefits. And to think of the millions of dollars of lost revenue is so sad. But it did explain the financial situation the facility was in and pointed to the ignorance of previous leadership.

I knew I needed to convince the board that a change had to be made in the therapy department. This was an unheard-of concept to my staff. No one defied the hospital. But I insisted that there were professional companies that did only long-term care, understood the reimbursement system, and made money for the facility.

In discussing the political sensitivity of changing therapy companies with my board of directors, it was decided that the hospital board and the Pleasant Acres boards should have a joint meeting. When the day came, I was a nervous wreck and knew it would be a huge stressor. My blood pressure rose to 101 over 108.

A joint-hospital nursing home board meeting was scheduled (the county also owned the hospital) to discuss the concept of changing therapy providers. The hospital board was shocked that such a thing could be considered. They wanted to know why.

The meeting itself was heated. I became particularly heated because of the presence of a guest the hospital administrator invited from the rural health cooperative. The cooperative actually employed the therapists and leased them to the hospital. The guest from the rural health cooperative kept telling lies, and I kept saying, "That's not true."

He insisted, for example, that his group did lots of nursing homes. In reality, his people knew nothing about Medicare or therapy, for that matter.

The meeting raged on.

Finally, in all his wisdom, the board chairman, Skip Walton, moved that the current therapists have four months to increase their revenue. He also moved that an independent audit be conducted to determine if the current therapists are doing an adequate job. The hospital administrator, Carrie Lewis, volunteered for the hospital to pay for it. Well, the nursing home couldn't afford it that was for sure. Also it was an unbudgeted expense.

A couple of weeks later, Carrie came in with two potential auditors, and together we agreed on Schneider and Associates.

Their expert consultant therapist from Utah called me to schedule the audit. She was a professional, and I let her know the reason the audit was being requested. It was explained that there were concerns about underutilization of therapy resources. She, the consultant, came in for two days and reviewed a sample of charts. When she interviewed Debbie, she also became aware of the ignorance of the current therapists. She scolded Debbie and reduced her to tears.

Her outcome was as expected. The hospital therapists had woefully let down the residents for decades and underserved their needs. When the doctors learned that outcome, they were immediately enraged that I would criticize a component of the health-care delivery system in Red Bud. The concern was not for the health care of our people; it was for the comfort and continuity of the status quo of their little world. They stated that all I wanted was money- their money.

After the outcome of the audit came out in the paper, the doctors wrote me a series of nasty letters and said terrible things about me. I was just trying to grow revenue and meet my resident's needs. They were furious that I would try to discredit any aspect of local health care. They believed that I was taking revenue out of the county. They also wrote letters to all local dentists, and eye doctors and podiatrists stating that I was also planning to bring geriatric specialists into the facility.

The fact is, I was planning just that. It was more convenient for the residents and spared the facility the expense of transporting the residents to these appointments. The contract company billed the pay source directly sparing the facility the burden of billing.

The most advantageous service we bought in was x-ray. Falls or injuries occur most in the middle of the night. This meant that the maintenance man would have to be awakened and brought in to transport the resident to the ER. He was always paid overtime for this, another expense for the facility. Sometimes it was bitter cold weather. The contract x-ray people came right in and took the film. They made a CD of the x-ray that could go right to the hospital with the resident if further treatment was needed.

The doctors said they wanted their own radiologist to read the x-ray. Plus they claimed they had no computers to read the film. I found this hard to believe.

The hospital charged three times what the contract company did and the nursing home had to pay for it since the hospital did not bill Medicare or Medicaid.

Since the doctors insisted on their own radiologist it was necessary to wait until he had outpatient hours at the hospital clinic. This meant that sometimes a resident with a fracture could wait days without being treated. This caused additional suffering for the resident: no cast, no immobilizer, no pain meds.

It was also a regulatory violation and when we were surveyed resulted in a citation and possible fine.

Eventually the doctors wrote their orders that the x-ray had to be taken at the hospital ER.

The hospital had a thriving outpatient clinic source of revenue. The contract company was cutting into their revenue. The hospital charged the nursing home a $100.00 dollars when a resident had an appointment. We could not bill Medicare because the hospital did first so the hospital was paid twice. Plus again the facility also bore the cost of two-way transportation.

Following the joint meeting, between hospital and nursing home boards when the county chairman ordered the therapy audit, the hospital therapists made no changes in their operations. The board had given them four months.

During the four months the board gave them to increase business and revenue they made no effort to do so.

The search was on for a new therapy company. My department heads were ready to go, having decided this was the right path. But the county board was going to be a harder sell. These companies were very professional and had been around a while. So gathering the data was not hard to assemble. The therapy companies were motivated to get the business. They prepared very professional and complete reports. They projected, with hard facts and case studies, that they could get us more than $300,000. It turned out that these were conservative estimates. It was more like $500,000. So the bottom line was soon in the black. But obtaining a new therapy company took a lot out of me. My blood pressure was constantly high.

Additionally in 2012, the facility did not need the referendum money. We were very fortunate to increase our revenue. My plan was to use the unused referendum funds to make long-needed capital improvements, such as a new roof and heating and cooling pipe replacements. There was increased revenue and excellent management.

The paper printed an article that the board supported the administrator. "Douglas has taken a great deal of heat during her time as administrator most recently for the number of employee dismissals that have occurred in recent months." Yet when I was hired, I was instructed to enforce disciplinary policies that these people had been breaking for years with no consequences.

This meant that I didn't have to make all the expense cuts I had anticipated. There were cuts to make because we still had a number of poor practices. Most of them were tied up in the union contract. Things that never really did happen were a reduction in office supplies. The kitchen was overstaffed, but the dietary manager simply would not schedule fewer hours.

*Things come apart so easily when they have been held together with lies.*

—Dorothy Allison from *Bastard out of Carolina*

# CHAPTER 5

## MABEL AND HER TERMINATION

During my first summer at the facility, Mabel Bitters, the bookkeeper, took time off to have some kind of voluntary hip surgery. While she was gone, I seized the opportunity to examine her books as well as her practices. I quickly discovered a variety of glaring problems and poor practices. Much to my horror, Mabel had run her tax-preparing business on the clock and out of her office at the facility. Meanwhile, she was collecting excessive overtime. Her clients were mostly staff who also met with her while on the clock. The administrators who knew of this pretended it didn't exist. This excessive use of overtime had been going on for years. Mabel was known to either lose her temper when confronted or, if that didn't work, she would break down in hysterical tears. Several people told me that she was so intimidating they just didn't want to deal with her. They were cowards who did not want an unpleasant confrontation.

The reason she had been hired out of the facility kitchen to be the facility bookkeeper was on the premise that she originally was an accountant. On a hunch, I called the registrar at her college for verification of her degree. Turned out she never graduated and had lied on her application. In most companies, that is grounds for termination. Yet she was allowed to continue working.

While this was all going on, Mabel had set up the worst accounting system that made some things virtually untraceable. The auditors who came in for their required annual audit just took her word for the numbers. When something didn't balance, she just told them she was working on it. There was never any follow-up in subsequent audits. She kept a tight hold on all accounting matters so if something was irregular, it couldn't be discovered.

She had been there a long time and had developed trust with the auditors since the same ones came every year. Because of this rapport the auditors grew complacent. When the numbers didn't reconcile she would say she was working on it and would type this in her account notes which was also repeated in the audit report. I told this to the board members but surprisingly this response sufficed.

I also discovered that some residents were receiving both a pension and Medicaid. Mabel kept all the pension money for the facility. It helped her financials look better. I believe she excused some people parts of their private pay bill. This was part of her overall strategy to ingratiate herself to persons in the community. However, that was fraudulent.

I would liken Mabel to the facility Godfather. She granted favors to various people and later collected favors back. These actions all helped convince the public that she had much power. They could bypass the administrator and director of nursing, and she would help them. After all, the administrator and director of nursing were busy, and she could handle whatever the problems were.

During the time she was out on medical leave, the leadership team decided to rearrange offices. There was nothing personal about it. No other staff member complained about the move. When she returned from leave, she raised a huge ruckus that she had not been consulted about the office I had selected for her. She actually blubbered that she needed an office with a window because her body temperature had trouble regulating itself. I told her I would accept her resignation at any time.

Long-term staff reported that years ago she had obtained her large office on the third floor because of its many windows. Meanwhile, the only office left was a tiny used-to-be storage room. She had this huge office. Mabel wanted everyone to cram into a small office so she could be comfortable. Mabel had a phone. They all had to share one.

The goal of moving Mabel was to make her office into the charting room. Of course, previously, they could not swap offices because Mabel contended she needed a window to help her regulate her body temperature.

My plan was to move her into the former HR office so resident families had access to her for answers to their question about their bill. Of course, this office had no window either. So another huge tantrum ensued. She recruited Dr. Brown to write me a nasty letter about her medical needs and how just after having surgery she should not be stressed. He also stated that I should value her as a good employee.

That letter came to my home, which I consider unprofessional.

In the end, Mabel ended up in the office next to me. It made it much easier to monitor her.

As for the ongoing issue of overtime, she needed two full days on the weekend to organize her new office. All overtime, of course. And that was when she would visit residents to give them assurances that she could take care of all their problems. No one else could or would.

Then I took a few days off. I asked the human resources manager to monitor Mabel's behavior. She did.

Based on the report from Candy I had believed that Mabel should be disciplined. However, there was no way I was going to do it without permission from the county board.

The chairman of the county board checked with three county attorneys, and they all agreed terminating her met the "just cause" standard.

Mabel was truly a detriment to Peaceful Acres. She had been abusing so many rules for twenty years. She failed to bill properly, which left the facility short of revenue. She had also excused people from their bills, which left them obligated to her, like the godfather. She was occupied with gossip.

Then came that fateful day that turned out to be the beginning of the end for my tenure at Peaceful Acres. One day, Mabel came bursting into my office waving papers in my face, clenched firmly in her fist. She was visibly upset. From her computer she had been able to access several of my personal emails to others wherein she was mentioned in a negative light. She was so furious over this that she had made copies of my personal emails and then confronted me with them.

"They're about me!" she exclaimed.

What led to her termination was that I had asked the board, at a closed session, to support me if I disciplined her for reading my emails and her excessive overtime. They agreed they would support me. Prior to that closed session, the agenda had noted that Mabel would be discussed. It is customary for agendas and minutes to be accessible to the public.

When we adjourned to go into closed session, she assumed she could come in. I stopped her at the door and said she could not come in. She became angry and tearful.

She said again, "You are going to talk about me!"

I said, "Perhaps, but it needs to be private."

She was terribly angry.

This was the first time I saw what she could do by assembling a posse, including residents. After the session ended and the board reconvened to our usual agenda, I noted Mabel speaking to people, riling them up and crying. She believed she was going to be fired and tried to garner resident support. Later, I was informed by department heads who were not in the closed session that Mabel was whipping up the crowd to defend her for her upcoming termination.

Even later in the evening, a resident refused to go to bed. She was so worked up about "what would become of us if Mabel were to leave" that she could not sleep but cried continuously. This was documented in the chart of the resident.

This was emotional abuse and against the law according to the home's regulations, and according to compassionate caregiving. The staff easily influences the residents. Taking advantage of this vulnerability is the work of abusive people.

The only board member available to act as witness for Mabel's discipline meeting was Rhoda Rondell. She agreed to come in.

Prior to meeting with Mabel, Rhoda said, "That woman will never stop making trouble for you until you fire her."

Jolene and Candy heard Rhoda say it. She was right. That woman would never stop making trouble for me. It wasn't until I terminated her that the real trouble started.

I called Mabel into my office with Rhoda and Candy as witnesses. I told her that she had no right to read my emails.

"But they were about me!" she shrieked. Narcissists believe that the world revolves around them and everyone should adjust to their behavior.

She refused to be seated and invaded my personal space. Candy took notes. Rhoda and I were just horrified at her comments, her attitude, and her body language. She insisted she had rights.

I said, "This is a disciplinary session, not a court. You have no rights that are being violated."

By then, I was so afraid of her, and I think Rhoda was too. Candy was used to her and just kept writing. My write-up for her said the emails were taken off the fax machine. Mabel thought it crucial that the documentation be changed. I replied that I could do it, but it wouldn't change anything. This infuriated her further. I could not have her going out to the staff and telling them who knew what. Since it was late in the afternoon, I told her to go home and calm down. She huffed and puffed but did go.

Mabel was disciplined and sent home because she became so hostile and vicious. The next day, Skip and our attorneys told me to fire her because of her insubordination and to stress the likelihood that she would claim workman's compensation.

I called her and asked her to come in. In typical Mabel fashion, she needed to take control of the situation. She said she needed to make some phone calls first. I could not allow that, so I called her back but got the answering machine. I left a message that said she had to come in, that I wanted her keys, and that she would receive a letter of termination regarding her insubordination. When she called me back, she was threatening and said abusive things to me. She threatened both me and the county with a lawsuit. Her real abusive comments came later when she filed her grievance and started writing letters to the editor of the local newspaper.

She finally came in and I told her she was terminated.

The next day, I had Bobby from maintenance deliver her personal stuff to her house. She refused it and said she had the right to pack up her own stuff. She called Skip and reminded him of a precedent that had been set that allowed the terminated employee to pack up her own stuff. So Skip arranged for Mr. Bernie Schmidt to observe while she packed up her stuff.

Of course, Mabel availed herself to the county process of appealing any discipline. The first hearing is held simply before the grievance board, and they render a decision at that meeting. The board members denied her grievance.

The second hearing was held in the county boardroom. Mabel had her usual mob there. She must have called a hundred people. She gave a lengthy testimony that included many irrelevant "facts." She complained that I slammed doors and I was all over the building and when someone came looking for me she couldn't find me. Most of what she rambled on about had nothing to with her termination, which was the purpose of the hearing. At one point, I commented that it was difficult to find people to witness her termination. The common response was that "she ruins people." When that was stated, her crowd burst out laughing. She went through the crowd shaking hands and thanking them all for coming. It was her day.

Board members then retired to a room across the hall. During the hearing and waiting for the board to return, there were insults and catcalls directed at me.

The board returned and once again denied Mabel's grievance. Mabel's gathered cohorts shouted and booed and wanted to string me up like in the Old West.

Unbeknownst to me, Mabel Bitters and her tribe of disgruntled employees had people believing all they said about the facility and me. They even had the doctors convinced that the care was worse because of me. This was a big following and very vocal.

*There is no ammunition as great as gossip.*

—Ernest Hemingway

# CHAPTER 6

## MABEL'S REVENGE

After being terminated, Mabel's first effort at retaliation was a rash of nasty letters to the editor about how horrible and incompetent I am. And she recruited relatives and other incompetent, terminated employees to sign letters she herself had written. For weeks, I was trashed and vilified in the local *Democratic Gazette*. It always hurt, and it always made me cry but only because it was so unfair and so untrue. And there was nothing I could do that wasn't a sin. Everyone said she would burn herself out, and it would all die down. My staff and the board continued to support me.

Mabel and her posse were not breaking any libel laws; just expressing their opinion. But I had no idea to what extent the people of this community wanted to hear and believe dirt on anyone. This is especially true when the target is an outsider such as me. But the letters were wicked and hurtful, since most were published in the paper.

What is interesting is that the paper published all of them. Some of what they wrote was true, and some was not. I remained reticent, not wishing to dignify her remarks.

For a while, the letters were a weekly occurrence. These nasty personal attacks took their toll on my blood pressure and my emotional well-being. There were days when I cried and others when I took a drive just to decompress. Yet I faithfully went to work each day. That was my duty. Many of the letters were written by Mabel, and she would get others to sign them. The paper had a policy that a person can only write one letter a month.

Articles about Mabel were also published outlining her abuse by me and her plans to hold grievance hearings and get her job back. I was never interviewed for my concerns or my side of the dispute. Her arguments had nothing to do with the insubordination or the viewing of my emails and confronting me about them.

The editor of the paper also printed many articles about Mabel's termination. Each one presented Mabel as a victim of a wicked administrator. There was never a hint that Mabel may have deserved the termination.

The fact that the newspaper press releases were printed without even interviewing me was a surprise. Higher-quality journalists always attempt to validate reports by interviewing the opposing party.

Mabel's behavior reminds me of a lady who was known by her priest to gossip. The priest took a feather-filled pillow and asked the woman to accompany him to the roof. He gave the lady a knife and told her to cut a hole in the pillow. The feathers then flew out and blew everywhere. Then he told her to gather up the feathers and put them back in the pillow. It turned out to be a most difficult task. He said, "Well, that's what gossip is too. Once you spread it around, it cannot be put back."

*Indifference and neglect often do more damage than outright dislike.*
— J. K. Rowling, *Harry Potter and the Order of the Phoenix*

# CHAPTER 7

# A COMMUNITY OF ENABLERS

There was a resident, Mr. Sommers, whose spouse, Ethel, had made it no secret that she wanted her husband dead. No one knew what to do except take our usual good care of him. We had reported her to Adult Protective Services, and social worker Jackie Crist agreed he was communicative and could have a quality of life.

Ethel was furious with this news and said that it was nobody's business. One of the board members said she had enough money to pay for him for years.

The drama began when Ethel was able to convince Dr. Spaulding to stop all of his medications. The doctor agreed. Again I called Adult Protective Services. Jackie Crist spoke to the doctor and reminded him that some of those meds, such as insulin were necessary for his well-being. She threatened the doctor with elder abuse charges.

He was angry but he told Ethel he would find a doctor in Millville who would service her husband at the assisted living facility to which she wanted to move him. I called the assisted living and was assured by the director that they could care for Mr. Sommers.

One day Ethel and her daughter snuck up the back stairs and somehow got him out of the building and into the car. He is unable to walk. Only the third floor nurse knew about it. They told her that they were taking him to visit the assisted living center. The nurse accepted this and was not concerned. I did not know that he was missing until 11:00 p. m.

The regulations and the facility have protocols for missing residents. The doctor must be informed. When I called Dr. Spaulding to report that he was missing the doctor already knew about it. He had found the doctor to follow him in the next county. The resident was in the next county out of county law enforcement's jurisdiction. New regulations also required me to notify local law enforcement so I called the chief of police. He called Ethel at home and she told him I was holding her husband against his will so she had taken him out and that he was in a safe place. The chief was satisfied with this.

Ethel also called the state surveyors. She reported that I was holding her husband against his will. She also reported that the family stated they wanted him moved to an assisted living. I responded that he was total care and not suitable for that facility. The director of the assisted living also called the state surveyors. She reported that I was holding the resident against his will and that I had sworn at her.

The surveyor called me and told me that I had better fax certain parts of the medical record to the assisted living which I did. Generally when there is a facility transfer the receiving facility visits the resident and evaluates whether or not the resident is suitable for their facility. This did not happen. It surprised me that he would be accepted without an evaluation and requesting medical information.

In three weeks, the resident was dead. I called Dr. Spaulding to report the death, and it seemed he didn't even care. The police also didn't care. It seemed as if this man did not matter to anyone.

One of the facility nurses who attended the same church as Ethel reported that the gossip around the church was that Ethel had finally gotten rid of him. Ethel had made statements to many that he was a financial burden. The facility's social worker had told me that a few years ago Ethel had taken her husband home stating she would care for him herself. During that time the social worker charted that she had admitted to dragging her husband across the yard when he could still walk and dragged him up the stairs. It also was charted that Ethel had admitted to pushing him down the stairs. The whole care plan team had heard these admissions. I was appalled.

I went to visit the attorney for county Human Services. He stated that he had known Ethel all of his life since he grew up on the farm next to hers. The couple had six grown children who were all afraid of Ethel. At that time he said there was nothing he could do.

In two weeks the surveyors came in to investigate a complaint made by Ethel and the director of the assisted living. They believed that I had sworn at the director. The facility was cited for not having an appropriate discharge plan. It was cited at a level G which is fineable. One would have to read the entire survey to understand how serious this was.

Mabel was a good friend and advisor to Ethel. Later I discovered that Mabel had also called the state.

*A people that value its privileges above its principles will soon lose them both.*

—Dwight D. Eisenhower

# CHAPTER 8

## A Special Board Meeting Regarding a Complaint

Our survey process began in the spring. A survey is a federal mandate. We received an immediate jeopardy cite on a resident who had been in the facility for years. For various medical reasons, he had a wound on his coccyx, which is a triangular bone at the base of the spinal column, which would heal and then reopen and heal again. His history was all over the chart. Yet the wound was open at the time of survey, and we received an immediate jeopardy citation.

Regarding one of the immediate jeopardy cites, the facility retained an attorney to aid us in an informal deficiency dispute resolution at a price tag of $9,000. We lost.

When the surveyors came back, they did not clear us and found another immediate jeopardy citation. It was based on the fact that a resident had sores on his toes. When we sent him to the hospital, they diagnosed it as cellulitis because that is a qualifying admitting diagnosis. He was on his way to gangrene, though. His primary doctor had written a prescription for antibiotics with a stop date, which the facility honored. His doctor had expected the nurses to call her for a renewal order when it again became necessary. They did not do it.

It was the daughter of this resident who asked for a special closed meeting of the facility board. She believed that all the things that happened to her father's health were purposeful neglect directed by me.

A special board meeting, therefore, had been called into closed sessions. The first topic was based on a complaint from the Seth Bonner family who had already called the state to report us and had inflicted on us an immediate jeopardy citation and several fines. In addition, it put us out of regulatory compliance again.

That request by the daughter of the resident had been the basis for the citation at last survey. She had requested the entire chart of the resident, her relative for whom she was Power of Attorney. She wanted to talk to the board, me, Helen, and Cindy. Dr. Smith had been invited because she had written the order to stop the antibiotic. Peaceful Acres board attorney and members were there along with Lester Bonner, younger brother of the resident, a visitor brought by the family (a nurse at another nursing home in an adjacent county) and the brother of the complainant. The family wanted me to be fired over this. The state had already cited us and fined us over this incident.

The nurse invited by the family was from Maple Grove and was most inappropriate and never introduced to me, so I do not know who exactly she was. Her name was Charlene Anderson, according to Cindy. She was incredibly nasty with all of her remarks.

At one point, she said, "I am concerned about the facility because of the remarks this administrator has made." Clearly, it was a personal attack.

At that point, I had not really had a chance to say much at all. Skip stopped the visitor and said he wouldn't tolerate a personal attack. (The complainant had complained to all the board members.) I was unaware of this. It turned out to be the conduit for revenge.

Sometime during the meeting I asked that visiting nurse, if her administrator knew where she was. There was much general conversation at this point, so I could not hear the full reply, but she was smirking and said, "Of course she does," but I could not hear the rest.

Helen said, "This has nothing to do with Olivia, our administrator, or with administration. This is a nursing issue and my responsibility."

The following day, I asked Helen if she thought the real purpose of the meeting was to get rid of me personally. She said, "Yes," and that is why she retorted the way that she did.

During the course of the meeting, Helen started crying because she said mistakes have been made. "These problems are long-standing. They will not correct quickly."

The nurse had said to Helen, "You didn't deserve to be put into the middle of all these problems. Are you getting bad orders from higher up?"

Lester Bonner started in about the fact that in two years, thirty-five people were no longer employed at the facility. I was angry, and I said that no one had been terminated without legal advice that it was appropriate.

Skip also said to him that I had more people to fire too. He also brought up the history of the facility's Ruff Riders.

Dr. Smith got her shots in by way of personal attacks. She commented that she was afraid for her license and the other doctors were too. She commented that in the last two years things had become so much worse at the facility.

Bernie Schmidt said, "What are you talking about? Things have never been better. They are making a profit."

Dr. Smith snottily replied that they might be financially better, but in every other way, they are worse.

She said, "By working with Peaceful Acres, we doctors are putting our licenses on the line."

That was a personal attack. I put my license on the line. Dr. Smith was always out of compliance with frequency of physician visits specified in the regulations. Dr. Smith wrote the stop order for the antibiotic that was the lynchpin of their complaint. The doctors had written orders every year that got us citations. They were very old-fashioned and refused to modernize or conform to the regulations.

In another effort to malign me, the complainant spoke of Dorothy Barnes. She had said that Dorothy Barnes was the best nurse ever and kept families informed of all things. Helen said that Dorothy was very good at speaking to families but not anything else.

I interrupted and said she was a terrible nurse.

Many of the families thought Dorothy Barnes was the best nurse ever. (She was not.) This family was one of them.

All the doctors thought she was great too. I once investigated Dorothy for telling a family member lies and basically throwing Helen, the director of nursing, under the bus. When I interviewed Dr. Emmitt about it (Dr. Smith's husband), he lied to cover up for her, and then he quickly called her and told her there was a target on her back. Barnes told many staff about his warning that reported her statements to me. I was unable to follow through with discipline because of his statement. Because of their hatred for me, a doctor in the practice preferred a rotten employee over me and betrayed me. And it was done with lies.

Dorothy was of retirement age and quickly retired. There was no target on her back. She had worked over thirty years at the facility as an LPN and had not changed or modernized or done a thing to grow professionally.

*Loyalty and devotion lead to bravery. Bravery leads to the spirit of the self-sacrifice.*

—Morihei Ueshiba

# CHAPTER 9

## SKIP WALTON'S RECALL

Meanwhile, Mabel had drummed up support to get Skip Walton recalled. She had been unsuccessful in getting rid of me, so she went after Skip.

The candidate she drummed up to run against Skip was poor at best. He slept through their debate, and his answers to questions from the audience were childish.

The facility department heads got together, and I filed some paperwork. Then I emailed the local paper about taking out an advertisement encouraging folks to vote for Skip because he was so supportive of us.

The night before the election, my department heads and I called everyone in the district. On the day of the election, Mabel gathered yet another mob, and they lingered at the courthouse. How disappointing it must have been to them that he was reelected.

*Three things cannot be hidden: the sun and the moon and the truth.*

—Buddha

# CHAPTER 10

## CHIEF OF POLICE JED POORMAN

One day, I received a call from Jed Poorman, the chief of police. He stated he needed my help with a case he was working on. And so I willingly went to see him, wanting to be helpful.

When the chief of police interviewed me, he recorded the conversation, which I knew they did. What I have never seen happen before was that conversations from the tape were released to the papers and published in the paper. It just added to my embarrassment. Because I thought we were friends, I didn't even know it was legal to disclose something that could be possible evidence should it end up as a court case.

I ended the statement with a flip remark, saying, "Are you going to take me to jail now?" A lot of people thought that was hilarious.

A year earlier, Mabel had sent a complaint to the state alleging that I had violated the law by using a county computer for personal gain. The state officials did not want to bother with it, so they passed it on to the local police.

County Board Chairman Skip Walton told me that he had contacted all three county attorneys who all agreed that no real law had been broken.

In trying to get to the bottom of things, Police Chief Poorman also talked to a former social worker for the facility. Her name was Sherrie

Johnson, and she said I had declared that if Skip didn't survive the recall election, I was going to lose my job. She was particularly credible because she had quit her job and had not been fired. She painted me as paranoid and selfish. As a boss, I had never done anything to her but be kind. Yet she wanted to get on the train trying to run me out of town. I don't know why she did it, other than that she was part of the Red Bud culture.

The email I had sent to the paper about running the ad was done on a county-owned computer. This was something I never even thought about. (Jed Poorman had a copy of the email. How did he get it?) I had talked to Jed, and he knew it was off the website Zimbra. He had called me and had asked me what I was doing on a certain to day in July 2011, and I did not remember. The state had had the complaint for a year and kicked it to the local cops. Jed wanted to get me in trouble. He did his investigation and took it to the District Attorney Renee Ward, who is married to Dr. Brown, who is not a supporter of me.

I had other documentation elsewhere. They had cooked up some statutory violation. They had sent a letter to all sixteen county board members hoping to get rid of me. Skip had talked to Buster Wade, corporate counsel who said no state law had been violated. Skip also recalled situations where Gloria Green, the county clerk, had sent emails to many people in the county, including Skip and my human resources manager, asking them to vote for her. Nothing was done to her.

There were others too. But it was my violation of the policy that made the headlines. At the board meeting, I had told them that I just didn't think of it as a crime. I would never deliberately commit such a crime. Mr. Schmidt and the board, however, insisted that a memo be put in my file telling me never to do such a thing again. I know he was just trying to protect me in case anyone accuses them of favoring me and not following through. At that time, the board remained supportive and encouraging, and this was reported in the local newspaper.

Jed Poorman and I had had another discussion after the debate between the candidates at Skip's recall proceedings.

I had seen Bonnie, a nurse who had allowed a resident to die and later lied about it. I saw her leaving as I was coming. I pointed her out to my husband as the nurse who had let that happen and I wasn't quiet about it. Well, she called Jed, and he called me and proceeded to scold me for telling my husband who she was. So I felt angry and that my right to free speech had been violated. But the nurse wanted me charged with disturbing the peace. He was inclined to do it, but there were no real grounds.

*Even in a minority of one ... there was truth and there was untruth.*

—George Orwell

# CHAPTER 11

# My Lawsuit

Not long after my discussion with Jed Poorman, I received a summons and charges in the mail. In other words, whoever typed my letter and summons had basically told the whole town. Everyone knew before I did. June Peterson is the clerk of court, and she had obviously no control over her staff or participated with them.

So I realized I needed a lawyer. I called the county board chairman who I believed to be my friend because he had always supported me. He gave me the name of a strange guy who had retained a very good lawyer; I called this attorney and made an appointment.

In the end, I did not appear in court. My lawyer did. I was very afraid that Mabel would be present with her mob.

While all this was going on, what I didn't know was that Chairman Walton had been talking to a lady from up north and that she was to serve as the new administrator to replace me and be administrator of both the hospital and the nursing home. He had led me to believe that she was a consultant. She was a replacement—for me! He did this to help me think I would have support.

*People will believe a big lie sooner than a little one, and if you repeat it frequently enough people will sooner or later believe it.*

—Walter Langer

# CHAPTER 12

## STAFF SABOTAGE

When Dr. Rothman, the facility's medical director, would come for quality assurance meetings, she would publicly berate Helen and me. I usually left crying. My team would tell her things had never been better, but there was no convincing her.

Meanwhile, the state kept coming in for surveys and revisits, and Helen and Cindy and I suspected that staff was sabotaging the process. They would disappear at mealtimes and make med-pass mistakes—anything to get rid of me by having a bad survey. The senior nursing staff fed the residents. So the residents were not neglected in any way.

Early last spring, I had heard Rose Greer reprimanding Bertha Brandice. She said, "You know perfectly well what is going on in this building." I wondered what that meant, having known these people and their vicious determination for revenge. But I blew it off. I knew Mabel was out there spreading lies and dirt. What I did not know was that Mabel was out there holding meetings in her home, hosting telephone chains, and writing letters to anyone she considered to be of local influence.

This group of people accepted innies in the community and want outies gone.

One former employee who could have been fired for absenteeism and poor performance over the twenty years that she had worked there never was. I finally fired her for just cause. Later on, her letter to the editor indicated that she was fired because she had breast cancer. She wasn't even diagnosed until weeks after her dismissal.

Then came the day that all the staff "knew" that Skip and I had been taken away to jail in handcuffs. Cindy asked me about it. I said it just wasn't true, and I had no idea how that rumor got started.

We were commanded to have a directed plan of correction on the last survey. It wasn't uncommon. I was to hire a consultant, and the instructions were to interview staff and make recommendations about improving the facility. A lot of staff purposefully didn't do their jobs during the survey to make it a poor one.

The consultant's investigative report was not a nice one. Many of my staff reported that I showed them no respect. Department heads said things in a nice way, but it wasn't enough.

*In a time of universal deceit telling the truth is a revolutionary act.*

—George Orwell

# CHAPTER 13

# BOARD MEETING WITH MOB

Then came another meeting of the board. We had a closed session scheduled to discuss the report the consultant brought as part of the directed plan of correction. When it arrived, my concern was that it required the consultants to interview staff and find out what they thought the problems were in the facility. The report she wrote was devastating. The staff and the resident families riled up by the Mabel Bitters posse had been writing the state with complaints about me. And they had been writing multiple letters to county board members. The recipients believed these letters, and the doctors had also called the state with complaints about nursing care and about me. The readers of these letters believed them. I had no idea as to the contents, but they must have been very terrible. It's like it was a delineation of every sin and mistake I had ever made. Some of the comments in the report prepared by the consultants contained quotes from the letters they wrote. Other un-named persons' comments that were made were printed in the report. The supervisor accompanied the surveyors on their last visit and reported to the Director of Nursing that they had received over 200 complaints about me.

Also in attendance at this meeting were the Regis consultants who had written the document for the directed plan of correction. Before meetings begin, people from the public are invited to make a statement. Mabel had gathered another large group believing I was to be fired that night. One of the local doctors read a statement denouncing me and calling for my termination. It was very humiliating.

Then we retreated to a closed session. The Regis people were as hostile as some of the board members and were complaining that too many people had been negative toward me. I was paying them to present an unbiased report. They were not able to be unbiased. Mabel had programmed them well. None of it was true, but it sounded true to the listeners.

Lester Bonner had berated me at many public meetings. Usually, Skip would reprimand him publicly, and I would hear about it later. I asked our attorney who was also there if anyone was terminated without me discussing it with our attorney. This was the first time he responded that no one had been. The meeting was a humiliating experience all the way around. My accounting manager stuck up for me. She stated that I was a good boss and that this was just a character assassination. She resigned within the next week.

We adjourned back to the regular meeting and agenda. The meeting was finally adjourned.

Mabel's mob was yelling and screaming, and they felt cheated that they had not witnessed my final humiliation. The last article to appear in the *Democratic Gazette* was the one about how a crowd had gathered at the facility. The accounting manager resigned. She had said repeatedly to me that she had never seen such behavior in a workplace.

*The best people possess a feeling for beauty, the courage to take risks, use discipline to tell the truth and the capacity for sacrifice, ironically it is their virtues that that make them vulnerable. They are wounded; sometimes destroyed.*

—Ernest Hemingway

# CHAPTER 14

## My Last Day and Termination

The day after the meeting, I was summoned back to the office. I knew that I was going to be fired as soon as Cindy called and gave me the message. She sensed it as well. Together we had seen a lot of such things over the years. Health care is a ruthless business.

Mike Schuster, Bernie Schmidt, and Skip Walton, all board members, were at this special meeting. I knew they were going to fire me. They put me on administrative leave for three months and said they would pay my health insurance, giving me time to find another job. The board agreed to pay my benefits. This was a relief and helped me feel better.

However, about two months later, they told me that they would not keep their promise of three months of administrative leave. I asked why and was told that there was public pressure not to pay me when I wasn't working. There was lots of precedent showing in the county history of people who were on administrative leave and paid.

A couple of weeks later, early in November, I received a call at home from the facility's labor lawyer. He told me that a special meeting was going to be held later in the week. During the meeting, I was going to be fired if I did not hand in my resignation beforehand. He wanted me to sign a document promising I would never disclose any of this to anyone. And it made me very angry. One of the stipulations was that I could not sue the county. I did not need to sign anything.

My letter of resignation would be enough. It was. I turned it in just a couple of hours before the meeting and, thus, ended my relationship with Georgia County.

But he hasn't got anything on.

—Hans Christian Andersen, *The Emperor's New Clothes*

# CHAPTER 15

## WHAT I HAD DISCOVERED

So many people are familiar with Hans Christian Andersen's fairy tales. A favorite of mine is *The Emperor's New Clothes*. In this story, the author describes a very rich and most arrogant emperor. One day, two swindlers showed up and introduced themselves as weavers. They claimed that their clothes had a wonderful way of becoming invisible to anyone who was unfit for office or who was unusually stupid. The emperor thought if he owned and wore such clothes he would be able to discover which men in his empire were unfit for their posts.

When the weavers were finally done with their task, the emperor made a grand march through his city showing off his new clothes. Everyone could see that he was naked but no one wanted to speak up in case that might prove that they were indeed stupid. It was only a little child in his innocence that commented that the Emperor wasn't wearing any clothes.

Well, I was that little child in the town of Red Bud. I was the first and only person to recognize the fact that the Peaceful Acres employees, the town doctors, and the facility board members, indeed, "had no clothes." They simply paraded around generation after generation proud of their non-accomplishments in the health-care industry, and the whole town, in total ignorance, continually applauded their efforts.

As that little child, it was I who was hushed by the townsfolk. I was the one to be stripped of my job and my good name. And I was the one made to feel stupid.

*So we beat on, boats against the current, borne back ceaselessly into the past.*

—F. Scott Fitzgerald, *The Great Gatsby*

# CHAPTER 16

## Now as I Look Back

As I look back at my time at Peaceful Acres, I realize now that I had never run a nursing home where such fraudulent activities not only existed but were tolerated. The usual and customary practice when things are not going right in a facility is to contract with an outside agency to bring in-house specialists in to see the residents. The cost savings are enormous, and the resident doesn't have to leave the facility. The facility is excused the cost of a van to transport and a driver paid overtime to do it.

Also, during my tenure at Peaceful Acres, the staff and doctors became comfortable with sending emergency cases out at 2:00 a.m. The facility had received citations for it. Funny thing was, when surveyors asked about these situations, people like Bobby Jones and Beth Wright couldn't remember who rode in the van. Not surprisingly, surveyors seemed to think that a critically ill patient should have an RN, not just the on-call maintenance man driving to the hospital. We were cited for this.

When I would bring up that the facility staff and doctors had mishandled things over the years, this caused much argument in the facility. Many staff members said I was making it up and trying to get people in trouble. The doctors from the Brown-Spaulding practice came to the quality assurance meetings at the facility and often scolded us. They implied that if we were going to call the 911 people that much, it would wear the EMT's out. They simply could not be bothered that much.

The policy that came out of all of this was changed to require calling 911 only in emergency situations. Alice Jensen, the previous DON, tried to enforce it. But there was a fair amount of ignoring it, which was common with every change that was attempted in this facility. The staff blew it off and did what they had always done.

When I first entered the building, there was a horrible survey citation concerning physician notification according to regulation. The regulations were specific as to when to call the doctor. In this case, the man was deteriorating fast. The RN on duty did not call the doctor since the patient didn't tell her he was getting sicker. The third shift nurse, however, did note it and called Dr. Smith.

She gave her standard answer: "Whatever the family wants." It took too much time to locate the family. The man died. The facility received an immediate jeopardy citation and fines.

Since my arrival, I can say that it is my belief that every survey has had physician notification as a citation. The policy had been changed, and the staff had been in-serviced, sometimes even by consultants the state forced us to hire. While it is true that some of the worst nurses no longer work at the facility, the issue still remains. The doctors still remain hard to reach by phone, not responding after multiple tries. And when they gave a call back, they would scold the nurses for disturbing them.

None of these are excuses. The nurses still need to step up and do their job, but they don't.

As the industry has changed, the facility has not. No one prior to my arrival recognized the necessity or enforced the regulatory changes.

*In three words, I can sum up everything I've learned in life: it goes on.*

—Robert Frost

# CONCLUSION

All of the people who I thought supported me during my time at Peaceful Acres have since evaporated from my life. Sometimes in my sadder moments, I wonder if they ever were my friends.

The most hurtful thing to me was that the board, which had always supported me, in reality probably never did. They simply could not accept my success.

Mabel is in the process of suing the county right now. She has more rights than I ever was afforded. I found that excessively unfair. I remain convinced that the county will pay her off with a large sum.

If I could get a job, it would help to remove my accumulated personal debt and overwhelming depression.

I go nowhere in this town for fear of seeing some of the people who have behaved cruelly toward me and participated in my ruined reputation.

My resume will now reflect a termination. My resume already has several gaps in employment. At this time, I have no desire to even renew my nursing home administrator's license.

It's difficult to start over in your sixties. This whole episode has seriously affected my health. I am frequently falling. My blood pressure is very high. My thoughts are often jumbled. I was recently hospitalized for dehydration and electrolyte imbalance. I have lost almost forty pounds, and as a result, all of my clothes are too big. Some of them have actually fallen off while I was in public. Normally, I would snicker at such a thing since seeing someone's pants fall off would be funny.

I continue to try to move on. While it is difficult, it is necessary. The people who have been cruel to me not only have abandoned me but also have nothing to say to me.

So I invite anyone with a similar story to contact me.

I wish to emphasize that not all the people who live here in Red Bud are mean. They simply are products of a mean culture. They know many people who are from other places, and from them, they have learned wonderful things. So numbers of them are polite and thoughtful. I am really grateful when someone is kind.